Todo sale cuando quieres

All gets out when you love/want

Kars Karsen

Hacè tiempo para sentir, los pensamientos vienen despuès
Make time to feel, the thoughts come thereafter.

Hola!. Soy Erik Kars Karsen Gleiss, nacì y me criè en Uruguay, y vivo en Holanda. Escribì este librito el domingo 15 de enero del 2023.

Hallo!. I am Erik Kars Karsen Gleiss, born and grown up in Uruguay, and living in Holland. I wrote this booklet on sunday 15 of january 2023.

Te mando saludos, aunque no te conozca.
I send you greetings, even though I don't know you.

© 2023 Kars Karsen. All rights reserved.

No part of this book may be reproduced, stored in a retrieval system, or transmitted by any means without the written permission of the author.

AuthorHouse™ UK
1663 Liberty Drive
Bloomington, IN 47403 USA
www.authorhouse.co.uk
UK TFN: 0800 0148641 (Toll Free inside the UK)
UK Local: 02036 956322 (+44 20 3695 6322 from outside the UK)

Because of the dynamic nature of the Internet, any web addresses or links contained in this book may have changed since publication and may no longer be valid. The views expressed in this work are solely those of the author and do not necessarily reflect the views of the publisher, and the publisher hereby disclaims any responsibility for them.

Any people depicted in stock imagery provided by Getty Images are models, and such images are being used for illustrative purposes only. Certain stock imagery © Getty Images.

This book is printed on acid-free paper.

ISBN: 979-8-8230-8063-7 (sc)
ISBN: 979-8-8230-8062-0 (e)

Print information available on the last page.

Published by AuthorHouse 02/06/2023

authorHOUSE

Contents

Todo sale cuando quieres i

Getting on with nature 57

    ❖ UFO'S 107

    ❖ Ancestor 110

    ❖ Writing 111

    ❖ Present and future 112

Living for the love 113

Frases de Kars Karsen

Sentences by Kars Karsen

Vivir significa estar contigo
to live means to be with you/yourself

No estàs solo cuando vives contigo
you are not alone when living with yourself

No perdones la maldad, sì a los malhechores
don't forgive the evil, do so to the wrongdoers

El idioma español es fàcil de aprender
the spanish language is easy to learn

Vivir para que todos disfruten
live for all to enjoy

Salir de tus cabales no es tan malo
to go out of your sanes is not that bad

La vida se relaciona contigo
life relates with you

La claridad es lo que necesitas
the clarity is what you need

Cantar como pàjaros no molesta a nadie
to sing as birds doesn't bother anybody

Comer rico me gusta todos los dìas
to eat tasty pleases me every day

Quitate los problemas como te quitas las ropas
remove the problems as you remove your clothes

Salir para volver
go out to return

Pedì ayuda para salir del paso
ask for help to muddle through

Pasear significa estar contigo
to walk means being with yourself/you

Entremeterte con otros no te ayuda
to intrude others does not help you

Saludar es abrirte
to greet is to open up

Los animales te saludan tambièn, acaricialos si te dejan
the animals greet you too, caress them if they allow you

Caminar no se aprende, comer tampoco
to walk is not learnt, to eat neither

El frìo te hace bien cuando lo necesitas
the cold does good when you need it

El volver es un tema meticuloso
to return is a meticulous issue

Tenè cosas que te ayuden a organisarte
have stuffs that help you get organised

Los pies son manos que acarician el piso
the feet are hands that caress the ground

Comprà cosas que te ayuden
buy stuffs that helps you

El camino tiene un orden
the path has an order

No te desesperes
do not despair

Lo chiquito vale doble
the tiny worths double

Contar es cantar nùmeros
to count is to sing numbers

El papel envoltuorio es voluntario
the wrapper paper is voluntary

Comè lo que quieras, siempre y cuando sea vegetal
eat what you want, always and only it is vegetable

Derretir es lo que tù me haces
melt is what you do to me

Comprà lo que es facil de comer
buy what is easy to eat

Seguir el camino es escuchar y ver
to follow the path is to hear and to see

El amor es real
the love is real

Seguì las imàgines y pensamientos que te vienen
follow the images and thoughts that come to you

Hacè un poco de esfuerzo para agarrar lo que quieres
make a little bit of effort to grab what you want/love

Lo vegetal no necesita reclames
what's vegetable does not need advertisings/claims

Da vueltas para conseguir lo vegetal
spin around to get what's vegetable

Seguì tu camino despaciosamente
follow your path slowly

Decidì estar entre lo que te gusta
decide being in between what you like

Agradecè lo que recibìs
thank what you receive

Las flores tienen colores para divertirte
the flowers have colors to amuse you

El camino de otros no es el tuyo
the path of others is not yours

Sentàte para aclarar los pensamientos
sit down to clear up the thoughts

Las formalidades no son necesarias
the formalities are not necesary

Lo que nos damos mutuamente es exclusivo
what we give mutually is exclusive

Dale acciòn a tus pensamientos
give action to your thoughts

El caminar te otorga buenos pensamientos
the walk grants you good thoughts

Recogè las basuras pequeñas que encuentres al caminar
collect the trashes that you meet at the walk

No necesitàs una mesa para comer
you don't need a table to eat

Otros siguen sus caminos
others follow their path

Abrì las puertas enfrente tuyo
open up the doors in front of you

Un poquito de esfuerzo te completa
a little of effort completes you

Cantar es vivir notoriamente
to sing is to live notoriously

Los niños estàn para ayudarte
the children are to help you

El control nos vuelve locos
the control drives us crazy

Todo en la naturaleza tiene mensaje
everything in the nature has a message

No repitas lo que dijiste, decilo en forma nueva
don't repeat what you said, say it in a new way

Todo puede salir ràpido, como un parto fàcil
everything can get out fast, as an easy birth

Los minerales ayudan mucho, aunque parezcan parcos
the minerals help much, even though they seem speechless

No pares tu fluìr
don't stop your flowing

Cocinar al tanteo produce las mejores comidas
to cook spontaneously produces the best meals

La palabra espontànea es la màs natural
the spontaneous word is the most natural

No dejes caer lo que te ayuda
don't let fall out what helps you

Abrir algo nuevo te invita a hacer algo nuevo en tu camino
to open something new invites you to do something new in your path

La naturaleza verde no llama la atenciòn
the green nature doesn't call for attention

Usà tus propias verdades
use your own trues

No guardes lo que no usàs màs
don't save what you don't use any longer

Crear tu propio mundo es un don natural
to create your own world is a natural gift

El cuerpo te ayuda en tus emprendimientos
the body helps you in your undertakings

Contà cosas como te vienen las cosas, sin fitrar
tell things as the things come to you, without filtering

Usamos los colores que nos atraen, siempre hay otros colores atractivos
we use the colours that attract us, there are always other attractive colours

Usà tus propias palabras, que son las mejores
use your own words, that are the best

Lo vivido està dentro tuyo, aunque te parezca olvidado
what lived is inside of you, even though it seems forgotten to you

Vivir para los demàs es vivir para tì mismo
to live for the others is to live for yourself

No fuerces las cosas cuando no es necesario
don't force the things when it is not necessary

Lo simple es lo directo
the simple is the direct

Guardà algo para despuès
keep something for later

El camino tiene sus propias vueltas
the path has its own turns

No cambies lo que està bien
don't change what is good

El pelo es el toque final del cuerpo
the hair is the finishing touch of the body

El escribir te reconfirma lo sentido
to write reconfirms you what's felt

Descansar es volver a vivir de nuevo
to rest is to return to life again

Veo todavia a algunos de mis amiguitos de infancia
I still see some of my little friends of my childhood

Amar es seguir viviendo
to love is to keep living

La pelota de la vida sigue sin parar
the ball of life keeps on going without stop

Pararse significa erguirse
to stand up is to raise

El alimento de la vida es tan variado como el de las verduras
the ailment of life is as varied as that of vegetables

El marco de la vida no es rìgido
the framework of life is not rigid

De izquierda y de derecha, todo jugador se hace bueno
of left and of right, each player gets good

Todas las cosas vividas pertenecen al mismo flujo
every thing lived pertains to the same flow

La naturaleza da sin pedir nada a cambio
the nature gives without asking anything in return

El sol resplandece en los niños escolares
the sun shines in the school children

Tabarè no fuè el ùltimo indio charrùa, su sangre vive en muchas personas
Tabarè was not the last charrùa indian, his blood lives in many persons

El negro no me da màs miedo
the black gives me not fear anymore

Escribir para no leer
to write to not read

Dejàte crecer un poco las uñas y los pelos
let your nails and hairs grow a little

Comer lo que uno quiere es una ventaja de estos días
to eat what someone wants is an advantage of these days

Las nubes lloran en lluvias
the clouds cry out in rains

No tengas miedo de ser ridículo
don't be afraid of being ridiculous

Tallar es quitar lo que no es necesario
to incise is to take out what is not necessary

Romper el pasado no se puede
to break the past is not viable

Las cosas al revès tambièn funcionan
the things the other way around also do they work

En mi niñez habìa una enciclopedia infantil llamada "Lo sè todo"
in my childhood there was a childish encyclopedia called 'I know everything'

Traer desde lejos cosas complica la naturaleza
to bring things from far complicates the nature

Vivir es dejar vivir sin màs
to live is to let live without further ado

Atraer es un don para sobrevivir
to attract is a gift to survive

Cuando me siento en casa no necesito salir
when I feel at home I don't need to go out

A las plantas hay que tambièn rociarlas
the plants have to be also being sprayed

Tomar agua caliente sòla tambièn me hace bien
to drink warm water alone also does me well

Cuando empezaste una marcha, seguì adelante
when you started a march, go ahead

Usà lo que tenès
use what you have

Las legumbres son las màs baratas fuentes de proteìnas
the legumes are the cheapest source of proteins

No chequees lo que ya sabès
don't check out what you already know

2 pequeñas caminatas al dìa son suficiente ejercicio
2 short walks a day are enough exercise

Vivir simplemente es vivir justamente
to live simply is to live justly

El juzgar es para juzgados, no para la gente
to judge is for courts, not for the people

El espìritu no sufre enfermedades
the spirit doesn't suffer illnesses

Dar para recibir no es gustoso
to give to receive is not tasty

El amor puro es el que todos tenemos
the pure love is what we all have

Hay todavìa mucho para cantar, dijo el payador
there is still a lot to sing, said the minstrel

Escribì inmediatamente lo que pensàs, si te parece necesario
write out immediately what you think, if it seems necessary to you

No cierres las puertas
don't close the doors

Preparàte todo lo mejor
prepare yourself all the best

No tengas miedo, la dicha es buena
don't be afraid, the bliss is good

Arreglà las cosas como te funcionen lo mejor
arrange the things as they function the better for you

El sentimiento indìgena vive
the indigenous feeling is alive

Las plantas te esperan en tu casa
the plants are waiting for you at your house

Las escaleras son un buen invento
the ladders/staircases are a good invention

Hay gente que son vividos
there are people that are lived

Cada cosa en su momento
every thing in its moment

Me reconforta ver como algunas cosas salen
it comforts me to see how some things come out

Andà a la cita en tiempo
go to the appointment on time

Lo que estaba escondido resulta ser mucho màs de lo pensado
what was hidden results to be much more than what was thought-out

Superticiòn no es mala
superstition is not bad

No corrigas lo que escribiste
don't correct what you wrote

Avanzà hacia la naturaleza
advance towards the nature

La lluvia no molesta
the rain doesn't bother

Si te sorprende algo, no te alarmes
if something surprises you, don't be alarmed

Tus proyectos son lo gustoso de tu diario vivir
your projects are the tasty of your daily living

Influir a otros es intervenir en sus vidas
to influence others is to intervine in their lives

Vivir es dejar que las cosas buenas sucedan
to live is to let the good things happen

Cosas buenas suceden cuando la naturaleza en tu interior se manifiesta
good things happen when the nature in your inner manifests itself

La naturaleza interior es individual y siempre buena
the inner nature is individual and always good

Hay chistes que no se pueden traducir
there are jokes that can not be translated

Esperà hasta que tu naturaleza te mueva
wait until your nature moves you

Algunas personas comen poco, sobretodo ancianos
some people eat little bit, above all older people

Es fàcil dejar que tu naturaleza se manifieste
it is easy to allow your nature to manifest itself

Hacè lo simple
do the simple

Los proyectos tienen su duraciòn propia
the projects have their own duration

Para sentir tu naturaleza no tenès que prepararte
to feel your nature you don't need to prepare yourself

Tranquilidad gustosa
tranquility tasty

Colgà tu abrigo, pero no tu vida
hang up your coat, but not your life

Amigos son todos aquellos con los cuales no necesitàs hacer una cita
friends are all those with whom you don't need to make an appointment

No te remuerdas de lo que hiciste
don't prick afflict yourself for what you did

Lo cientìfico y lo espiritual tienen que ir de la mano
the scientific and the spiritual have to go hand in hand

No repitas exactamente lo que ya dijiste, usà nuevas palabras
don't repeat exactly what you already said, use new words

El arte de vivir es estar atento a lo que tenès que hacer ahora
the art to live is to be careful to what you have to do now

Hacer lo que tenès ahora te proteje de la ansiedad
to do what you have now protects you from anxiety

Hacer cortito y al pie son los escalones de la escalera del dìa
to do short and at the foot are the steps of the staircase of the day

Siempre tenè fruta para enseguida comer cuando sientas ganas
always have fruit to right away eat when you feel like it

No necesitamos màs comer ni usar animales
we don't any longer need to eat nor to use animals

Paz viene cuando sentimos la paz de nuestra naturaleza interior
peace comes when we feel the peace of our inner nature

La naturaleza ha estado en paz desde siempre
the nature has been in peace since ever

No te escondas de nadie
don't hide from nobody

Recalentar la comida no es tan bueno como parece
to reheat the food is not as good as it looks like

Lo vegetal crudo es lo màs natural
the raw vegetable is the most natural

Tanto los animales como los humanos siempre han encontrado soluciones para vivir
so much the animals as the humans have always found solutions to live

La vida es una pelìcula sin tìtulo
the life is a movie without title

La naturaleza no es estática
the nature is not static

Todo lo vegetal comunica en silencio
everything vegetable communicates in silence

Todo lo vegetal se expresa sin movimiento
everything vegetable expresses itself without movement

Buscamos usar colores porque los sentimos
we seek to use colours because we feel them

Nosotros tenemos brazos y piernas porque hay cosas que hacer
we have arms and legs because there are things to be done

Son 2 cerebros, el izquierdo y el derecho
they are 2 brains, the left and the right

La verdad de las cosas es la verdad
the truth of the things is the truth

Reìrte de ti mismo te ayuda
to laugh about yourself helps you

No tenès que acomodarte a la vida, la naturaleza te ha dado espacio
you don't need to accommodate you to the life, the nature has given you space

Elevate tanto como sientas
rise up so much as you feel

La ciencia usa la naturaleza para desarrollarse
the science uses the nature to develop itself

El cuerpo te ayuda a cumplir tu misiòn
the body helps you to accomplish your mission

Hay muchas teorìas y practicas, la naturaleza es una
there are many theories and practices, the nature is one

Hacè tiempo para sentir, los pensamientos vienen despuès
make time to feel, the thoughts come after

Amàndote amo a todo el mundo
loving you I love the whole world

Los tiempos pasados siguen existiendo, la esencia no ha cambiado
the past times keep existing, the essence has not changed

Todo lo que pasò no se fuè, aprendimos a querer como lo hacìan nuestros antepasados
everything that passed is not gone, we learned to love as our ancestors did

Lo que revienta es que no todos queremos paz, aunque sea nuestra naturaleza
what bursts is that not everyone of us wants peace, even though it is our nature

La salud la controla la naturaleza, aunque pensemos que es la ciencia
the health is controlled by the nature, although we may think it is the science

Viviendo en forma natural, la salud vuelve a tus manos
living in a natural way, the health returns to your hands

Quejarse es fàcil, reìr es màs fàcil todavìa
to complain is easy, to laugh is easier yet

Entra a la fuente de todo
enter to the source of everything

Vivir es abanderar a la vida
to live is to flag out the life

No te despiertes, sigue soñando
don't wake up, go on dreaming

Lo que necesita el alma es vivir el amor
what the soul needs is to live the love

Los lìmites los ponemos nosotros, el alma vuela encima de ellos
the limits are put by us, the soul flies above them

Vivir es lo que siempre queremos
to live is what we always want

La maravilla de la vida es recoger los frutos del amor
the wonderful of the life is to pick up the fruits of love

Comer para crecer, amar para crecer
to eat to grow up, to love to grow up

Salirte del tema de la vida te pone lejos de ti mismo
to get out of the theme of life puts you away from yourself

Los años pasan, la vida se queda en tus manos
the years go, the life stays in your hands

Complicaciones se arreglan cuando uno asì lo quiere
complications get corrected when one wants it to

La salida es la entrada
the exit is the entry

Entender sin saber exactamente lo que se dice
to understand without exactly knowing what is being said

La gente se entiende no solo a travès de palabras
the people understand each other not only through words

Sòlo se aprende cuando se quiere aprender
it can be only learned when it is wanted to learn

Aprender en la escuela de la calle significa aprender por experiencia
to learn in the school of the street means to learn by experience

Confià que la naturaleza interior va a finalmente ganar
trust that the inner nature is going to finally win

Probar significa abrir tus puertas a lo desconocido
to try means to open your doors to the unknown

Todo en cada ser viviente es ùnico en el mundo, aunque hayan similitudes
everything in each living being is unique in the world, even though there are similarities

La amistad ayuda, como tantas otras cosas
the friendship helps, as much as many other things

Poder elegir es un privilegio enorme
to be able to choose is an enormous privilege

Los pequeños momentos son los grandes momentos
the little moments are the big moments

Experiencias pasadas aclaran a veces lo que te pasa hoy
past experiences clarify sometimes what happens to you today

Vivir sin sentir no tiene sentido
to live without feeling has no sense

Las alergias no alegran
the allergies don't rejoice

No controles tu vida, dejà que la creatividad te guìe
don't control your life, let that the creativity guide you

Guardà los secretos compartièndolos
keep the secrets by sharing them

Incluye en tu vida a todos aquellos que te incluyen
include in your life all those that include you

El hogar lo tenemos adentro
the home is hold by us inside

Gracias!
Thanks

GETTING
ON WITH
NATURE

the inner and external natures
are parts of a native nature

KARS KARSEN

the inner and external natures are parts of a native nature

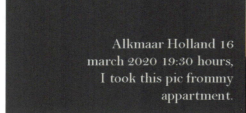

Alkmaar Holland 16 march 2020 19:30 hours, I took this pic from my appartment.

This booklet was completed in 11 days, from 4 january 2023 to the 14th. Another booklet was also completed in preceding few days: living for the love.

Erik Kars Karsen Gleiss was born and grown up in Uruguay, his mother's country, and lives in Holland, his father's country.

Following my family in Holland 2022.

Thanks! Gracias! Bedankt!

authorHOUSE®

ISBN 979-8-8230-8032-3

getting on with nature is living for the love

the inner and external natures are parts of a native nature

You need doing what you feel doing

. . . .

Dying must be an impressive experience too

. . . .

Leaving your nature is somehow abandoning yourself

. . . .

The 1st impulse is your nature's impulse

. . . .

The secrets and messages of live come and appear to you, pick
them up, keep them carefully and use them openly

. . . .

Wild animals do a tremendous effort to fulfill and employ their own nature, it is inspiring

. . . .

We still don't know all consequences of using and consuming chemicals

. . . .

Our body is the home of our own nature

. . . .

Do not stop the flow of your own nature

. . . .

Living simply gives the needed tranquility

. . . .

It is amazing how quickly children understand speaking

. . . .

Express your own nature, it's unique

. . . .

Have a colorfull living, colours provide happiness

. . . .

Inner nature provides satisfaction

. . . .

Free cooking is art

. . . .

Art is inner nature expressing through you

. . . .

Accomodate life to be able to express your nature

. . . .

Controlling others opposes trust and creativity

. . . .

Take time for yourself

. . . .

Bright colours fit young children, be a colorful young child again

. . . .

don't postpone any step within your flow

. . . .

The creativity of nature is countless

. . . .

Live and believe your inner nature

. . . .

Do not be dissapointed, a new flow will come to you

. . . .

When adjusted for monetary inflation, the controversial "Gone with the wind" is still the highest grossing film in history: imagine that! (from Wikipedia)

. . . .

Only you can tell the true story of your own life

. . . .

By overlooking spirituality you are missing insights

. . . .

Recognize when to stop

. . . .

The worldly "world" promises but doesn't deliver

. . . .

We get addicted by the chemicals in processed food and drink

. . . .

Discovering the nature within you is a science too

. . . .

Living is about materializing your spirit, your inner nature

. . . .

Do what you are good at, it is your contribution and fulfillment

. . . .

Let the past go, to start clean again

. . . .

let's all trust nature, without fearing the bad

. . . .

Keep perceiving your own inner nature, don't let that go

. . . .

The art of living is the recurring natural flow, every day

. . . .

You can't imagine what a new day will bring, feel prepared

. . . .

Feel prepared as a young student going to school

. . . .

Remember what did help you yesterday

. . . .

"come as you are" is the current song in my mind, by Nirvana
WEB SEARCH: Nirvana – Come as you are (lyrics)

. . . .

What an artist wants to tell you is never completely clear, is up to you to discover

. . . .

"don't break my heart" is the next song coming to my mind this early morning
WEB SEARCH: UB40 - Don't break my heart

. . . .

The one and only incredible you!

. . . .

Drinking 2 big glasses of warm water as my first breakfast

. . . .

Having enough time to write something

. . . .

The body will dwindle, the mind perhaps too, the soul happily enough will not

. . . .

Things happening remind you you need to take action, don't be surprised

. . . .

Our progression is being fuelled by our nature

. . . .

Protect what is good for you, carry on with it

. . . .

Develop your own style of live, that is also art

. . . .

Nothing teaches birds to sing nor to fly, they just do it naturally

. . . .

Look around you to develop your own philosophy

. . . .

Philosophy: "love for wisdom"

. . . .

Give your 'other side' a chance, that is what you didn't use

. . . .

Plant fruit trees in cities' streets, so that people can grab them

. . . .

There are 'melody' waves in poetry, and when writing spontaneously

. . . .

Feel what you eat before eating it

. . . .

We haven't progressed in all fields, work in progress

. . . .

Let yourself unfold during the day

. . . .

You don't need to read others to understand living

. . . .

What you do becomes a part of you

. . . .

We appreciate people that are pronounced

. . . .

Living is always work in progress, until it ends

. . . .

Inspiration comes to you almost unexpectadly

. . . .

Being good to others makes it

. . . .

Dedicate your living to your passion, if possible

. . . .

Sometimes you need to go back and forth to make things finally happen

. . . .

don't feel bound to always exactly follow your habits and routines

. . . .

Live for the sake of living

. . . .

Be the specialist of your own living

. . . .

Positive efforts are at last rewarded

. . . .

Making sometimes a joke helps relaxing

. . . .

My mother used to go singing to her work

. . . .

Be thankful for a person's good example

. . . .

Clean up your mind as much as you clean your house

. . . .

Home is both, your house and your inner nature

. . . .

A steady walking is a helpful and recovering exercise

. . . .

My father was very happy commanding a commercial ship

. . . .

Some people neglect receiving a compliment, some others become happy with it

. . . .

"the saga continues" (from Star Wars)

. . . .

A steady walk is helpful and good enough exercise

. . . .

Just simply saying "hallo!!"

. . . .

Do not kill animals

. . . .

don't prescribe others what to do or follow : freedom!

. . . .

Manufactured food is expensiever, eating then the natural raw ingredients of it

. . . .

"even geen ruzies jongens!" (for a bit no fight boys!)

. . . .

Walking through city parks as much as possible

. . . .

Go left, follow left, think left, left means creativity

. . . .

It is incredible what is happening

. . . .

Be carefull to survive

. . . .

When I was much younger I borrowed my senior accountant boss
a booklet with the "Murphy's Laws", when he returned it to me
later he was obviously not happy with what he had read

. . . .

Be silent when needed

. . . .

Decode into thoughts the messages you are receiving from inner and outside nature

. . . .

don't hurry when it is not needed

. . . .

Follow examples from others

. . . .

don't take these writings too seriously

. . . .

Preferably be in quietness when eating

. . . .

Analize what the specialist is saying

. . . .

Things may go faster than thought, may occur faster

. . . .

Be as strong as a yogi, it is possible!

. . . .

It is superfitial to stigmatise others

. . . .

Be open to hearing

. . . .

Remove some garbage on sidewalk when walking

. . . .

don't be indifferent, clean the environment

. . . .

nature's messages are specific and clear

. . . .

Walk with the ones you love, and also alone

. . . .

In too many places there are more streets for cars than
sidewalks for walking walkers, change the situation

. . . .

Preferably, don't walk the same path twice

. . . .

Preferably, don't repeat walking the same path

. . . .

Get what helps you

. . . .

Be ready for possible heavy occurrences

. . . .

Nature happens for your best living

. . . .

Put a limit to your daily spending

. . . .

People comfort other people

. . . .

I thought on you

. . . .

A young woman said "if I write everything, it can happen": agreed!

. . . .

When you receive a message, leave and go furthermore

. . . .

When following inner and outside nature living becomes simplified

. . . .

Nature helps you on your way

. . . .

We are/have antennas to nature's emmision

. . . .

Walk on the grass to connect!

. . . .

Reach home

. . . .

Enjoy the warmth that suits you

. . . .

WEB SEARCH: Although the sun is shinning – Fleetwood Mac

. . . .

When young children arrive to a beach, you don't need to explain them what to do. They find naturally out how to enjoy and what to do

. . . .

About ufo's: we all have passion for lights

. . . .

nature's timings are of the essence

. . . .

Crazy for lights

. . . .

The physical world is a question of the inner

. . . .

The physical world is divided by 2, the femenine masculine, left right

. . . .

Now a little bit of meditation, and physical recovery

. . . .

don't dominate the nature

. . . .

Nature opens and closes

. . . .

Be as flexible as an elastic

. . . .

Trust you have all necessary ingredients in you to succeed

. . . .

Living is also about materializing the spirit, the inner nature

. . . .

My mother used to walk singing to her work, always busy with ideas and initiatives, we very much enjoyed dancing together embracing each other

. . . .

My father was very happy commanding sea cargo ships, I occassionally
travelled with him during my childhood, when he was young he
wrote in one of his many photo albums: "the sea is calling"

. . . .

The inner and external natures are parts of a native nature

. . . .

A very little bit of formal meditation

. . . .

Meditation meaning:
perceiving your inner nature

. . . .

All-ways use and enjoy the inner and external nature

. . . .

Go yourself and vegan

. . . .

When invited, eat what you receive

. . . .

I want to activate *my nature*,
both inner and external

. . . .

Leave the green stay

. . . .

Please stay on budget

. . . .

don't ask for a special treatment, if not really needed

. . . .

Bring animals back to their wild

. . . .

Live according to what you say, what you act, and by your good intentions

. . . .

Follow your nature, no matter what don't overload your eating, stop when you feel doing so, and keep it fresh for the very 1st next time. Then you don't need a fridge

. . . .

You can use the juice of fruits to wash your body, and the liquid coming out of with water soaked oats to wash and rinse your hair. This works very well for me

. . . .

Eating raw vegetables help

. . . .

What is good for your internal body is also good for your external body, your skin and hair

. . . .

The sun's light radiation became dangerous only because and after we polluted our clean air

. . . .

Wash clothes by hand, as our progenitors did. Then you don't
need a washing machine. You don't need a dryer either

. . . .

The flow is an unexpected wave coming into you, and that you need to express

. . . .

Choose 100% natural food and clothes, it is possible

. . . .

Thanks very much for all the help that you and they give

. . . .

Nature has always been our matter

. . . .

Memory recreates what happened, memory is a progressive
creative tool, not just something static

. . . .

Live by your words, by your doings and by your good intentions

. . . .

Nature answers your questions and passions

. . . .

Nature develops and lives by it self own

. . . .

WEB SEARCH: Mystery magical tour – The Beatles

. . . .

The left side of our body is femenine, the right side of our body is masculine.

. . . .

Try to use both sides equally, specially your hands and your brains

. . . .

Left is a bit more creative, right is more of a controller

. . . .

Left more a receiver, right more a giver

. . . .

~ nature is love, love is nature ~

. . . .

Now some experiences and thoughts using more words:

. . . .

UFO'S

I was 16 when saw an ufo for the first time. It was near Punta Ballena in Uruguay, back in november or december 1973, when going for holidays on a evening in the car with the whole family of a friend, Jorge Rodriguez. It was dark and silent and I was looking at the outside when a strong white light surprised me, a light as you see in stadiums from underneath.

Then I thought how strange it was to see a light just above the lights of the entrance to the "Cabañas-cabins- del Tio Tom", slightly higher than us, even we were already on a slightly higher side of the road. And then I looked again .. then I saw it : there was a flying object suspended in the air of about 10 meters diameter, quiet and without moving. It was a round plate underneath, going cone onto the top of it, with strong white lights underneath, with in the middle body a very slightly fluorescent kind of metal like aluminium, then dark kind of windows on the top, and on the very top colorful basic bright lights consecutively circling like you see in a discotheque.

My friend and I started yelling to the father driving the car: stop, stop, STOP. The mother yelled loudly too "NO, NO"; the car carried on. When I looked again, the round cone floating in the air suddenly and quietely turnered 90 degrees staying in it's same position; the underneath strong white light then reached strongly our eyes.

Finally, the object started moving slowly, and always silently and peacefully, away from us, above the pine trees of the area, direction the near beach.

I then couldn't see it furthermore. We carried on our journey in silence.

I was told by a friend in my very early twenties, Alvaro Silva, that his parents were by then driving on a road by night, in the area between Punta Ballena and Punta del Este in Uruguay, when an effulging UFO landed very close to them at one side of the road. Their auto stopped abruptly, and a slightly effulging being came out of the UFO. It was slightly smaller than a human, looking like an older man and having a white beard, with a relatively bigger head than a human.

This being looked at them from the relative short distance, and they then telepatically heard something like: "don't ask me anyting, I don't know anything". Thereafter this being quickly and effortlessly walked into the bushes, and dissapeared.

Then the UFO left, and their car could start again. See a pic that I made in 2011 in Uruguay at the back cover of my other booklet "living for the love".

See also a pic that I made in 2020 in Holland at the back cover of this booklet.

Alternatives recently discovered and experienced by me

Before breakfast I drink 2 big glasses of fairly warm water. As breakfast I eat oats with 100% only peanut butter and bananas. More recently, and without my previous knowledge of it, I read and heard on the internet that oats were a main meal of vikings, and that peanuts with bananas a preferred meal of yogis is. Very nutritious and easy to digest, and it feels satisfying during hours.

I clean all my house, windows and dishes with a little bit of organic appel naturally-cloudy vinegar added to enough water. It disinfects very well, as it cleans your intestines when drinking a small sip of it with some water. You then don't need chemical cleaners. And is very unexpensive.

You could also use this natural vinegar in washing your gardments and all laundry, specially if they are 100% wool, 100% cotton of other natural materials. It should also work with polyester-with-cotton/wool materials.

I do a trickle of this vinegar in a water-sprayer bottle with enough water, and spray it where necessary at home.

By using organic virgin coconut oil I wash out my mouth, and brush my teeth. This oil, and specially this vinegar, are antibacterial and antiseptic.

Scrub the pulp and inner skin of fruits onto your skin. And use the liquid coming out of with water soaked or cooked oats mixed with a very little bit of this vinegar to wash and rinse your hair. You can use cacao powder and cinnamon powder as make-up, it feels warmish too.

Eating a lot of different raw vegetables directly helps your general health and reduces overweight fairly quickly. Lots of fairly warm water, and water directly from the tap, together with 2 daily good walks help(ed) me a lot too, recovering my general health. I was vegetarian since my 17, but since I became vegan my health improved furthermore.

What is historically known is that urine, also a strong vinegar, was used not only to wash clothes but also used by the romans to brush their teeth. It is now proven that the ammonia in urine bleaches the teeths and removes stains and tartars. WEB SEARCH: urine, het vloiebare goud van vroeger en nu – GreenPee (translated by me from Dutch: 'urine, the liquid gold from formerly and now').

Ancestor

My beloved little grandma Maria, mi querida abuelita:

I was holding her hand when she passed away, when I was 9. She used to pronounce me many old-time and practical wise proverbs, when in Uruguay.

She with her round silver spectackles, very long silver hair arranged in a bun, and very dark eyes. I saw her always and only wearing black dresses with printed small colorfull flowers on them; she weared black dresses since the day my grandfather died very long time before I was born.

She washed all loundry with her hands, cooked delicious and tastefull warm meals twice a day for the whole family of my professionally very busy aunt and uncle. And had solutions for everything. I was happy to help her once in a while by buying simple groceries like cookies and sugar, and by talking to her and by listening to her easy to follow language (she had been a school teacher).

I can simply not forget all of this.

Important to realise is that we all have native DNA in our body, regardless of the places where our family circumstantially and more recently is coming from. Very exciting and rewarding.

Writing

A daughter (a known writter) of a former boss of me (an englishman) wrote on the cover of a newspaper's magazine here in Holland, a few days ago: "Als ik schrijf kan alles gebeuren", translated by me as 'If I write everything can happen'.

The process of me writing my 2 booklets (I am not a writter) has been to immediately jot down observations and thoughts coming in, as literally as I possibly can. I don't like adjusting afterwards what I originally jotted down.

"she speaks!!" (Romeo about Juliette in an old movie, balcony scene, book written by Shakespeare)

Present and future

If you don't know or didn't learn facts, simply feel presume imagine how things happen(ed); these are also essential qualities and tools that we have to live naturally.

Technological devices and developments will not take over, nor replace, our beloved inner and external natures.

Note: I surprised myself writing this booklet.

Living for the love

Kars Karsen

live from, and express, the by you perceived inner and external natures

Circling bright lights are entities, zig-zagging ufo in the middle: I took this pic at the remote beach of Punta del Diablo in Uruguay, in february 2011.

This booklet was completed in 19 days, from 16 december 2022 to 3 january 2023. Another booklet was also completed in subsequent few days: getting on with nature.

Erik Kars Karsen Gleiss was born and grown up in Uruguay, his mother's country, and lives in Holland, his father's country.

Happy feeling summer in Uruguay 2012.

Thanks! Gracias! Bedankt!

ISBN 979-8-8230-8029-3

authorHOUSE

living for the love is getting on with nature

live from, and express, the by you perceived inner and external natures

the word "inspiration" comes from the old Italian word "inhale",
meaning: "the coming in of breath, inhalation"

---

other version is that "inspiration"
could mean "in spirit"

---

live for the love

---

animals are sensitive too

—————————————

care

—————————————

your nature says: I will always help others

—————————————

go vegan naturally grown, as much as by you affordable

---

we don't need anylonger domesticated animals as cows
horses pigs chicken, let's them put back into wild

---

hear what others say to you, there can be an usable message in it

---

keep in memory the good experiences you have/had

———————————

choose natural, when it is possible

———————————

make always time to feel nature

———————————

you do not need going to a forest to feel nature, nature is with you

---

rewilding domesticated animals like cows benefit ecosystems: WEB SEARCH: Rewilding europe making europe a wilder place

---

recreating aurochs, cow's ancestors: WEB SEARCH: Aurochs: back from extinction to rewild europe

---

recovery:
WEB SEARCH: Enigma - Return
To Innocence (Official Video)

———————————

recover what is yours

———————————

let people recover naturally

———————————

recover relations with friends and family you haven't talked to lately

———————————

let's remove all stigmas

———————————

don't impose your thoughts onto others, just share them, it is not about you 'winning'

———————————

nature leads you forward, not backwards

———————————

tranquility

———————————

the worldly 'world' put conditions, nature doesn't

———————————

nature's path gives you what you need and want

———————

grab! that

———————

turn onto nature's path

———————

go for 100% living it is now! 100%

———————

celebrate living

———————

feeling your own nature you may be alone but never lonely

———————

keep doing what works for you

---

relax! it is about your own living

---

living gives you opportunities to adjust your doings

---

simply adjust afterwards what you wrongly stated

———————————

don't underestimate the power of nature

———————————

without sharing love living becomes agony and dry

———————————

don't minimize your capabilities

---

each being has her/his own particularities

A very happy and healthy new year!

every-thing alive represents the whole nature

———————————

WEB SEARCH: una paloma blanca lyrics – george baker selection

———————————

every personal question and matter requires your taylormade answer

———————————

inspiration makes you happy

———————————

thank for inspiration received

———————————

every personal question and matter requires your taylormade answer

———————————

inspiration makes you happy

thank for inspiration received

surpass your own limits by following your nature

listening to
WEB SEARCH: 102.1 the edge the coolst music radio that I know

---

my wish for the new year is me to encounter it

---

good music and lyrics—+ WEB SEARCH: Waiting for the Sun - The Doors

---

a life comes to it's end, how will the new life be?

———————————

a year comes to it's end, how will the new year be?

———————————

every-thing in nature is our companion including the stars

———————————

we belong to nature

"the fruit of patience is very sweet" (Aristotle, 2.400 years ago)

---

stay open for everybody

---

state out your position in clear terms

———————

the inner nature gives you comfort in all circumstances

———————

speak out openly about your life, if someone wants to hear you

———————

bring the inner nature you have into practice

———————

regardless of how busy you are, keep your inner nature 'alive'

———————

the inner nature gives you comfort in all circumstances

———————

speak out openly about your life, if someone wants to hear you

---

bring the inner nature you have into practice

---

regardless of how busy you are, keep your inner nature 'alive'

---

trust you have within all natural
'ingredients' to succeed

---

wake up with best wishes for yourself and everybody

---

nature is already in total peace, let's then live according to nature

---

nature continually brings flows of inspiration, an inexhaustible
sources of inner and external natures

---

live your own way, not how others do, nor how you should

---

we are actors in nature's movie

---

nature lives in, and provides, peace

————————————

art and nature never repeat itself

————————————

live your own way, not how others do, nor how you should

————————————

circling bright lights in back cover are entities, zig-zagging ufo in middle:
I took pic in Uruguay 2011
Nieuwe Tweets bekijk
~ come To Life, for The Love ~

───────────────

nature lives in, and provides, peace

───────────────

art and nature never repeat itself

───────────────

move things to accommodate your understanding

---

nature is to enjoy and to show how to live life

---

sometimes it is something harder, sometimes it is easy

---

the connection to living is very strong

———————————

"heaven can wait" (film)

———————————

don't overload other people, understand their situation or position

———————————

recognize when you go out of your natural flow, and as soon as possible go back to it

———————————

choose for your own natural path

———————————

recognize shortcomings and mistakes committed in life

———————————

there is no time for nonsense in the world

---

cool off the 'heat' of worldly life

---

amplify the importance of preserving nature

---

love prevails

---

if you do something do it dedicatedly, otherwise do something different

---

let your nature expand your horizons

---

perceiving the inner nature (meditating) in bed

---

enjoy your dreams while awaken!
and while sleeping!

---

every new day brings new perspectives, experiences are different

---

it is endearing to see how nature performs it's own true
magic through people: seeds flourishing!

---

don't talk to control but to share

---

your inner nature remains intact! regardless of bad influences and experiences

---

thinking and acting strategically for own egoistic gain brings you away from your nature

———————

inspiration thoughts are the merit of your own nature

———————

if an inspiration thought comes into you, it happens for you to realise it

———————

to listen to another person you need to empty your mind

feeling love is as important as eating and drinking

believe in what you see and feel

reconciliation is an inspiring and warm experience

take steps to improve what you do around you

explain what you know, to help

the wishing to dominate is not a good characteristic in humans, and it is also not necessary

———————————

the magic of living is happening to me/you/us

———————————

hope provides rescue

———————————

inner and outside nature always welcome you

———————————

be a friend to your family members

———————————

be courageous and say what you have to say

———————————

be free from any kind of domination on you by any person

———————————

to-day you don't need to rush: holy-day
WEB SEARCH: Madonna Holiday Lyrics

———————————

help another at any cost you can afford

———————————

be really sincere when explaining what you have done: don't 'improve' the facts that ocurred

happy having some bright colors in clothes and at home

the 'world' and creativity of young children are simple and
amazing!, a real inspiration for grown up

family and friends are for you!

———————————

feeling the peace of a free day

———————————

there is a spiritual side to what we live

———————————

bliss comes sometimes into you almost unexpectedly

———————

asking and giving forgiveness for a mistake feels good

———————

there is native dna in our body

———————

observe well and listen well to the necessary signs you are receiving to move further

---

"nunca es tarde cuando la dicha es buena" (it is never late when the bliss is good)

"con libertad ni ofendo ni temo" (with freedom I don't offend nor I fear)
(quote by José Gervasio Artigas, liberator of Uruguay, dated 1815)

today a homeless helped me brilliantly! on the street

---

today wanting to resolve misunderstandings

---

clear lyrics:
WEB SEARCH: Tomorrow
Never Knows (2022 Mix)

---

discover the nature residing inside of you

---

correcting mistakes

---

living is beauty-full

---

young children are very funny!

———————

by activating your native roots and natural living, life's
routes and arts become visible and feasible

———————

"the force is with you" (from Star Wars)

———————

nature is what you really want, because nature is what
you are, because you pertain to nature

———————————

don't stop nature's flow in your daily life

———————————

the perceivable nature inside is not hiding

———————————

carry on getting your message through, and getting things done

———————

perceiving nature inside is very simple

———————

what you need from nature you already have

———————

keeping mouth quiet

————————

feeling breath moving

————————

seeing brightnesses with closed eyes

————————

listening to the sound of silence

—————————————

key is not making your habits a religion

—————————————

"the force is with you" (from Star Wars)

—————————————

nature is what you really want, because nature is what
you are, because you pertain to nature

———————————

don't stop nature's flow in your daily life

———————————

the perceivable nature inside is not hiding

———————————

carry on getting your message through, and getting things done

———————————

perceiving nature inside is very simple

———————————

what you need from nature you already have

———————————

listening to the sound of silence

———————

key is not making your habits a religion

———————

you live forward in the new generation

concentrate in letting the art of living happen

———————————

playing with children takes the breath and mind away

———————————

watching and hearing children play and speak heal

———————————

the right words come from the natural experience

———————————

you can realise life alone, follow your natural path

———————————

recognice the signs given to you

———————————

enjoy freedom

let the love experience take over every time

concentrate in letting the art of living happen

playing with children takes the breath and mind away

———————————

let the love experience flow throughout you

———————————

let the love experience take over every time

———————————

your nature is just in time

———————

your nature all-ways helps you, always

———————

the flow does not make mistake

———————

be happy perceiving nature that is inside of you

———————————

clean up your mind perceiving nature that is inside of you

———————————

choose for your true insight

———————————

do what your intuition tells you to do

———————

do not add anything to your intuition

———————

wake up to enjoy the gift of live&love

———————

give solution to the problem described

---

happy summer 2012 in Uruguay

---

the circling bright lights in the back cover are entities, zigzaging ufo far away in the middle of this picture taken by me in Punta del Diablo, east Uruguay in year 2011

---

meditating as a mix of what heared and what myself discovered

this is how i do my meditation

My favourite song out of my favourite album with favourite drawing: WEB SEARCH: closing my eyes (2013 remaster) Fleetwood mac – closing my eyes Fleetwood mac – then play on album

Listening when going out of bed and when going to bed:
WEB SEARCH: one hour relaxing birdsong: the nightingale

~ when all worldly lights turn off, your eyes remain my only light ~

Note: I surprised myself writing this booklet.

CPSIA information can be obtained
at www.ICGtesting.com
Printed in the USA
BVHW011435060623
665489BV00002B/10